You don't lose yourself

when you let go — you

find what's been

waiting all along.

— Rita Lynn Berry

Letting Go

A 40-Day Journey to Release and Renew

Rita Lynn Berry, Ed.S., LCMHC

Letting Go

A 40-Day Journey to Release and Renew

ISBN: 979-8-9912221-5-0

Cover and interior design by Rita Lynn Berry

Published by Mend n Muse Media, a division of NewVision Counseling and Consulting Services, PLLC

www.ritalynnberry.com

TABLE OF CONTENTS

WELCOME

Welcome, Beloved.

This 40-Day Journey is a sacred invitation to release what no longer serves, receive what your soul has been longing for, and return to the truth of who you are.

You are not here by accident. You are here because something within you is ready — ready to be free, to trust again, to loosen the grip on old wounds and walk gently into something new.

Letting go is not a one-time act, but a rhythm, a practice, a grace.

It is not weakness. It is wisdom.

It is not abandonment. It is alignment.

In these next 40 days, you will be guided — not pushed.

You will be invited — not forced.

You will be held — not judged.

You'll make space for grief, for hope, for breath.

Acknowledge the ache — it holds wisdom for your healing.

Bless the release.

And believe in the return.

Let's walk this journey together — one day, one breath, one release at a time.

With love,

Rita Lynn Berry

Author | Guide | Companion in Renewal

HOW TO USE THIS
GUIDED JOURNAL

This journal is your companion for a 40-day journey of personal release and emotional renewal.

Letting go is not a one-time decision—it's a practice of making space for healing, clarity, and peace. Through daily reflection and intentional journaling, you are invited to release what no longer serves you and step into the wholeness of who you are becoming.

Each day includes:

Opening Insight
A grounding thought or quote to begin your reflection

Theme Reflection
A message to guide your awareness and encourage emotional honesty

Prompt for Release
A focused question to help you examine what you're ready to let go

Truth to Carry Forward
A short affirmation or truth to hold as you move ahead

Lined Page
Space to write, explore, and reconnect with yourself

You may follow this journal in order or move intuitively through the days. Pause where you need to, and return when you're ready. Let this be a soft space to land, reflect, and rise.

Release is not weakness. It is wisdom.
Releasing what no longer serves makes space for what truly matters.

PART ONE

Letting Go of the Past

Before we can heal, we must name what needs to be released. In this first stretch of the journey, we begin to untangle from what was—regret, shame, old identities, and the stories we've been carrying too long. This is your sacred permission to lay it down, piece by piece, and open space for what's next.

Day 1 – Letting Go of What No Longer Serves

Light for Your Path

"You have to let go of who you were to become who you will be."
— Oprah Winfrey

Reflection

Life is a journey of constant evolution. Who you were five years ago, five months ago, or even five minutes ago, may not be who you need to be today. Clinging to outdated versions of yourself can keep you from stepping into your full potential. Just as a snake sheds its skin, you must shed the old layers to reveal the vibrant self underneath. Today, take a moment to consider what parts of yourself or your life are no longer serving your highest good. Be willing to release them, trusting that in doing so, you are making space for the person you are meant to become.

Affirmation

I release who I was to embrace who I am becoming, trusting that I am always growing into my best self.

Reflections with Grace

What are you ready to release that no longer serves you?

How might your life change if you let it go?

_____

_____

_____

_____

_____

_____

_____

_____

_____

_____

_____

Day 2 – Healing from What Was

Light for Your Path

"Holding on to anger is like drinking poison and expecting the other person to die."
— Buddha

Reflection

Pain and anger are powerful emotions. When someone hurts us, it's natural to feel betrayed, wounded, or even enraged. These emotions, while valid, can become toxic when we hold onto them for too long. Anger and resentment take root deep within us, affecting how we see ourselves and how we interact with the world. In reality, these emotions only hurt the person who carries them.

Think of anger as a hot coal. You clutch it, thinking it will keep you safe or give you the power to strike back. But over time, that coal only burns you. It scars your hand, your heart, and your spirit. Healing doesn't mean forgetting what happened or excusing the behavior of others. Healing means choosing yourself over the pain. It's about deciding that you deserve peace, even if they never apologize. Let go of the coal. Choose healing over hurt.

Affirmation

I release anger and resentment, knowing they no longer have power over me. I choose peace and healing for myself.

Reflections with Grace

What part of your story are you holding
onto out of habit or fear?
What truth feels more healing to embrace today?

_____

_____

_____

_____

_____

_____

_____

_____

_____

_____

_____

Day 3 – Letting Go of Regrets

Light for Your Path

"We all make mistakes, have struggles, and even regret things in our past. But you are not your mistakes; you are here now with the power to shape your day and your future."
— Steve Maraboli

Reflection

Regret can be a haunting companion, whispering reminders of choices we wish we could change. It shows up as a knot in your stomach when you think about that job you didn't take, that apology you didn't offer, or the love you let slip away. Regret ties you to the past, keeping you stuck in a moment that no longer exists. But living in regret prevents you from fully embracing the person you've become because of those very experiences.

What if, instead of looking at regret as a punishment, you saw it as a teacher? Every regret is a lesson in disguise, guiding you toward a wiser, more compassionate version of yourself. When you learn from your regrets and let go of the shame or disappointment, you free yourself to move forward. Today, look at one regret with fresh eyes. What has it taught you about who you are and what truly matters?

Affirmation
I release my regrets and embrace the lessons they've brought. I am free to create a new story for myself, one choice at a time.

Reflections with Grace

What do you need to forgive yourself
for to move forward?
How can you show yourself compassion today?

_____

_____

_____

_____

_____

_____

_____

_____

_____

_____

_____

Day 4 – Breaking Free from Shame

Light for Your Path

"Shame is a soul-eating emotion."
— Carl Jung

Reflection

Shame isn't just about what happened; it's about the story we tell ourselves afterward. Shame tells us we are flawed, that our mistakes define us, that we are unworthy of love, forgiveness, or acceptance. It latches on to moments of perceived failure and makes them part of our identity. The truth is, shame thrives in silence and secrecy. When we carry it alone, it festers and grows, wrapping us in a cloak of isolation and self-doubt.

Breaking free from shame starts with shedding light on it. Speak it aloud, share it with a trusted friend, or write it down in a journal. When shame is exposed, it begins to lose its power. You are not your worst moments. You are the strength it took to overcome them, the courage to face them, and the resilience to rise again. Remember, shame cannot survive empathy. Today, choose to speak kindly to yourself and let go of the shame that has weighed you down.

Affirmation
I release the shame I have carried and embrace the truth that I am worthy of love, forgiveness, and compassion.

Reflections with Grace

What shame-based belief about yourself are
you ready to release?
What truth can you choose to believe about yourself instead?

_____

_____

_____

_____

_____

_____

_____

_____

_____

_____

_____

_____

Day 5 – Untangling from Old Stories

Light for Your Path

"And after the fire came a gentle whisper."
— 1 Kings 19:12 (excerpt, *NIV*)

Reflection

We all have stories we tell ourselves—stories about who we are, what we can achieve, and what we deserve. Often, these stories were written by others, based on their perceptions or expectations. "I'm not smart enough." "I'm always too much." "I'll never be loved like that again." These narratives can become self-fulfilling prophecies, trapping us in cycles of fear and limitation. But what if those stories weren't true? What if they were just words, spoken at a time when you didn't know your own strength?

It's time to rewrite your story. You are not the words spoken over you. You are not bound by old definitions or expectations. Take a moment to identify one story you've been telling yourself that no longer serves you. How would your life change if you let go of that narrative and embraced a new one—one that reflects the resilient, brave, and worthy person you are?

Affirmation
Divine love whispers to me in stillness, and I hear it.

Reflections with Grace

What is a story you've been telling yourself that
no longer feels true or helpful?
Who might you become without that story
shaping your identity?

_____

_____

_____

_____

_____

_____

_____

_____

_____

_____

Day 6 – Moving Beyond Relationships That Hurt

Light for Your Path

"Some people come into your life as blessings. Others come into your life as lessons."
— Mother Teresa

Reflection

It's painful to admit when a relationship has become more harmful than healing. We hold on, believing that love means staying, that loyalty means sacrificing ourselves. But real love doesn't demand the betrayal of our own spirit. Sometimes, letting go of a relationship is the most loving act we can perform—for ourselves and for the other person.

Releasing someone doesn't mean you didn't care or that the relationship was without value. It means you value yourself enough to walk away from what no longer supports your growth. It's a recognition that your well-being matters, too. Letting go is not a failure; it's a courageous choice to honor yourself.

Affirmation
I am fully known and still fully loved.

Reflections with Grace

What relationship or dynamic has caused you pain but
still lingers in your heart or mind?
What do you need to release in order to reclaim your
peace and move forward?

_____

_____

_____

_____

_____

_____

_____

_____

_____

_____

Day 7 – Releasing Self-Blame

Light for Your Path

"You can't blame yourself for things you didn't know when you were doing the best you could with what you had."
— Unknown

Reflection

Blame is a sneaky companion that often comes disguised as self-reflection. It's that voice that says, "If only I had done things differently" or "I should have known better." We use it to hold ourselves accountable, but in reality, it serves only to keep us trapped in cycles of guilt and regret. Self-blame is especially harmful because it twists our past mistakes into statements of self-worth.

You are not your past choices. Every decision, every action, was made from a place of doing the best you could with the knowledge and emotional resources you had at that moment. Imagine speaking to your younger self. Would you chastise them for what they didn't know, or would you offer compassion and understanding? Today, let go of self-blame. Offer yourself the grace you would extend to a loved one, acknowledging that you did what you could. And now, with more wisdom and clarity, you're doing even better.

Affirmation

I release self-blame and choose compassion for myself. I honor the lessons of my past without allowing them to define my present.

Reflections with Grace

In what ways have you been holding yourself responsible for
things that were out of your control?
What would it feel like to offer yourself grace instead of guilt?

Day 8 – Letting Go of Unrealized Dreams

Light for Your Path

"Sometimes, we must let go of the life we have planned, so as to accept the one that is waiting for us."
— Joseph Campbell

Reflection

It's hard to let go of dreams that never came true. The career you didn't pursue. The relationship that never blossomed. The plans that never saw the light of day. We hold onto these unrealized dreams, believing they're still part of who we are. And sometimes, we cling to them because letting go feels like giving up on a piece of ourselves. But in reality, holding on to these dreams that didn't manifest can prevent us from seeing the possibilities that exist in the present.

What if those dreams, as beautiful as they were, were not meant to last? What if the delay or redirection was a gift in disguise, opening the door to something greater? Letting go of unrealized dreams is not about giving up—it's about making peace with what is and choosing to see new opportunities.

Affirmation
I release the dreams that no longer serve me and open my heart to new possibilities. I trust that what is meant for me will not pass me by.

Reflections with Grace

What dream or desire have you been holding
onto that hasn't come to pass?
What might open up in your life if you released it
with love, rather than regret?

_____

_____

_____

_____

_____

_____

_____

_____

_____

_____

Day 9 – Releasing the Need
to Be Right

Light for Your Path
"Sometimes being right is less important than being kind."
— Unknown

Reflection

The need to be right can create walls instead of bridges. It can turn simple disagreements into deep divisions and prevent us from seeing others' perspectives. When we cling to being right, we close ourselves off from empathy and understanding. But being right isn't the same as being happy or at peace. Sometimes, choosing kindness over being right can be the most powerful act of surrender.

Think of a recent conflict where you felt the need to prove your point. What would it have looked like if you chose to let go of being right and instead focused on understanding and connection? Letting go of this need doesn't mean you don't have valuable opinions or that your perspective isn't valid. It simply means valuing harmony over superiority. Today, in your interactions, try surrendering the need to be right. Choose to listen, to understand, and to connect.

Affirmation
I release my need to be right and choose kindness. I honor connection and understanding above all.

Reflections with Grace

When have you prioritized being right over being at peace?
What does it feel like to let go of that need and embrace
understanding instead?

_____

_____

_____

_____

_____

_____

_____

_____

_____

_____

_____

Day 10 – Trusting Your Inner Wisdom

Light for Your Path
"Your inner knowing is your only true compass."
— Joy Page

Reflection

In a world filled with external opinions and advice, it's easy to lose touch with our own inner voice. We look outside for validation, direction, and answers, doubting our ability to navigate life's challenges on our own. But deep within, there is a quiet, steady wisdom that knows what's best for you. This inner wisdom isn't loud or forceful; it's a gentle whisper that guides you toward choices that align with your true self.

Trusting your inner wisdom means surrendering the need for external approval. It's about quieting the noise around you and listening to that small, still voice within. When you honor your inner knowing, you build a stronger relationship with yourself. You learn to trust your own judgment and make decisions that honor your path. Today, take a moment to connect with your inner wisdom. What is it telling you? How can you honor it?

Affirmation
I release my need for external validation and trust my inner wisdom. I am guided by the truth within me.

Reflections with Grace

What is your intuition telling you about a current
situation in your life?
How can you begin to honor your inner voice more consistently?

_____

_____

_____

_____

_____

_____

_____

_____

_____

_____

_____

PART TWO

Surrendering to the Present Moment

There comes a point in the journey when we must stop clinging to what was and begin softening into what is. This section invites you to breathe, trust, and allow life to meet you here—in the now. Surrender isn't giving up. It's giving in to the truth that peace is found in presence, not perfection.

Day 11 – Embracing What Is

Light for Your Path
"Surrender to what is. Let go of what was. Have faith in what will be."
— Sonia Ricotti

Reflection

The present moment is often overshadowed by thoughts of what could have been or what should be. We live in a constant state of wishing things were different—different job, different health, different relationships. But this only leads to discontentment and resistance. When we surrender to what is, we aren't giving up or accepting defeat; we're making peace with reality. This peace gives us the clarity and energy to take meaningful action from a place of acceptance, not frustration.

Think of it like a river. You can stand in the middle, pushing against the current, getting nowhere, feeling exhausted and defeated. Or, you can let go and allow yourself to float, to be carried by the water, trusting it will lead you to where you're meant to be. Surrendering to the present moment is about accepting where you are right now, even if it's not where you want to stay. It's choosing to stop struggling and instead, flow.

Affirmation
I accept this moment for what it is and allow myself to flow with life's current. I trust that everything is unfolding perfectly.

Reflections with Grace

What parts of your current reality have you been resisting?
How might acceptance open the door to peace or clarity today?

_____

_____

_____

_____

_____

_____

_____

_____

_____

_____

_____

_____

Day 12 – Letting Go of Control

Light for Your Path

"You may not control all the events that happen to you, but you can decide not to be reduced by them."
— Maya Angelou

Reflection

Control gives us the illusion of security. We think if we can just organize everything and everyone, life will go according to our plans. But the truth is, control is often rooted in fear—fear of uncertainty, fear of loss, fear of things not turning out the way we hoped. The tighter we hold on, the more life seems to slip through our grasp, leaving us frustrated and overwhelmed.

Real power comes not from control but from the ability to let go. It's found in the courage to release our grip and trust that even if things don't unfold as expected, we have the strength to adapt and grow.

Affirmation
I release my need to control everything around me. I trust in life's natural flow and my ability to adapt and thrive.

Reflections with Grace

Where in your life are you holding on too tightly?
What would it feel like to trust the process, even
just a little more?

_____

_____

_____

_____

_____

_____

_____

_____

_____

_____

Day 13 – Finding Peace in Uncertainty

Light for Your Path
"Peace is not the absence of turmoil, but the ability to remain calm within it."
— Unknown

Reflection

Uncertainty can feel like standing on the edge of a cliff, peering into a foggy abyss where nothing is clear. It's unsettling, unnerving, and can bring out our deepest anxieties. Our natural instinct is to resist uncertainty, to scramble for answers and solutions, hoping to eliminate any unknowns. But what if we could learn to find peace right where we are, in the midst of the unknown?

Finding peace in uncertainty is about surrendering the need for immediate clarity and trusting that it will come in its own time. It's like being in the middle of a storm but finding shelter in the calmness within. The storm may rage outside, but inside, you are steady, still, and sure. Today, when faced with uncertainty, breathe deeply and center yourself. Remember that this too shall pass, and whatever is unclear now will eventually reveal itself.

Affirmation
I release my need for immediate answers and embrace the peace within me. I am calm, centered, and open to what life has to offer.

Reflections with Grace

What is one area of your life where you are seeking answers?
How can you begin to make peace with not knowing right now?

_____

_____

_____

_____

_____

_____

_____

_____

_____

_____

_____

Day 14 – Surrendering to Self-Compassion

Light for Your Path

"Be gentle with yourself, you are doing the best you can."
— Unknown

Reflection

We often reserve our harshest judgments and criticisms for ourselves. When we fall short of our expectations or make mistakes, the internal dialogue can become cruel and unforgiving. But self-compassion is an act of surrender—letting go of perfectionism and the unrealistic demands we place on ourselves. It's about recognizing that we, like everyone else, are human, beautifully flawed, and worthy of the same kindness we extend to others.

Imagine you're speaking to a dear friend who's struggling, blaming themselves for every misstep. Would you tell them to try harder, do better, or be more perfect? Or would you encourage them to be gentle, to forgive themselves, and to see their efforts in a kinder light? You deserve the same grace. Today, surrender the harsh self-talk and choose words of compassion and gentleness instead.

Affirmation

I surrender my self-judgment and choose self-compassion. I am doing the best I can, and that is enough.

Reflections with Grace

Where have you been hard on yourself lately?
What would it look like to meet that part of you
with compassion instead of criticism?

_____

_____

_____

_____

_____

_____

_____

_____

_____

_____

Day 15 – Trusting Life's Timing

Light for Your Path

"Trust the timing of your life."
— Unknown

Reflection

We live in a world that values speed, urgency, and instant results. We're taught that success means having it all right now. But true growth, healing, and fulfillment don't always happen on our preferred timeline. The path to meaningful change often involves detours, delays, and moments of waiting that test our patience and resolve.

Trusting life's timing means believing that everything unfolds exactly when it's meant to. The waiting isn't wasted; it's preparing you for what's to come. Think of a seed buried deep in the soil. It spends months in darkness, seemingly dormant, but during that time, it's building strength, forming roots, and preparing to sprout. When it finally breaks through the surface, it's ready to bloom. Today, release your impatience and trust that your season of growth is happening, even if you can't see it yet.

Affirmation

I release my impatience and trust the timing of my life. Everything is unfolding perfectly, even if it's not visible yet.

Reflections with Grace

What area of your life feels like it's not moving fast enough?
How might you shift from anxiety to trust in this
part of your journey?

_____

_____

_____

_____

_____

_____

_____

_____

_____

_____

_____

Day 16 – Surrendering to the Flow of Life

Light for Your Path
"You must learn to let go. Release the stress. You were never in control anyway."
— Steve Maraboli

Reflection

Stress often arises when we believe we must control every aspect of our lives—every detail, every outcome, every decision. But stress is the result of resisting life's natural flow. When we learn to surrender the illusion of control, we experience peace and lightness that come from trusting that life has a rhythm of its own.

Think of a leaf floating down a stream. The leaf doesn't worry about which rocks or branches it might encounter; it simply flows, trusting the current to carry it where it needs to go. Today, release your need to control every detail. Allow yourself to flow with life, trusting that wherever you are is exactly where you're meant to be.

Affirmation
I surrender my need for control and allow myself to flow with life's rhythm. I am at peace with where I am.

Reflections with Grace

Where in your life are you resisting what is unfolding?
What would it feel like to move with life instead of against it?

_____

_____

_____

_____

_____

_____

_____

_____

_____

_____

Day 17 – Allowing Yourself to Feel

Light for Your Path
"Feelings are much like waves, we can't stop them from coming, but we can choose which ones to surf."
— Jonatan Mårtensson

Reflection

In our fast-paced world, we're often encouraged to push through our emotions, to keep moving and stay productive. But ignoring feelings doesn't make them disappear; it only buries them deeper until they show up in unexpected ways—irritability, restlessness, or even physical illness. Surrendering to the present moment includes allowing yourself to feel what arises without judgment.

Give yourself permission to feel, whether it's joy, sadness, anger, or grief. Let the emotions come and go like waves. Some will be gentle and calming, others may crash with intensity, but all are temporary. Trying to control or suppress them only makes them stronger. Today, when an emotion arises, take a deep breath and allow yourself to experience it fully. Then, release it, knowing it's just a part of the greater flow of life.

Affirmation
I allow myself to feel fully and release each emotion as it comes, trusting that I am safe and supported in my experience.

Reflections with Grace

What emotions have you been holding back or avoiding?
What might those emotions be trying to show or teach you?

_____

_____

_____

_____

_____

_____

_____

_____

_____

_____

_____

Day 18 – Releasing the Fear
of the Unknown

Light for Your Path
"Everything you've ever wanted is on the other side of fear."
— George Addair

Reflection
Fear of the unknown can be paralyzing. It keeps us stuck in comfort zones that no longer fit, holding us back from taking risks that could lead to growth, joy, and fulfillment. But fear is just a doorway, a threshold between where we are and where we're meant to go. When we learn to surrender our fear and walk through that door, we open ourselves to a life filled with more courage and possibility than we ever imagined.

Today, think about one fear that's holding you back. What is it protecting you from? And what opportunities are you missing because of it? Acknowledge the fear, thank it for trying to keep you safe, but let it know it's time to step aside. Move forward with faith and courage, trusting that on the other side of fear is the life you've been longing to live.

Affirmation
I release my fear of the unknown and embrace the courage to move forward. I trust that what's waiting for me is greater than what I leave behind.

Reflections with Grace

What fears arise when you think about not
knowing what comes next?
How might it feel to welcome uncertainty as
part of your growth?

_____

_____

_____

_____

_____

_____

_____

_____

_____

_____

_____

Day 19 – Surrendering Perfectionism

Light for Your Path

"Perfection is not attainable, but if we chase perfection, we can catch excellence."
— Vince Lombardi

Reflection

Perfectionism can masquerade as a noble pursuit. It tells us that if we just try a little harder, work a little longer, or fix a few more things, we'll finally be "good enough." But perfectionism isn't about striving for excellence; it's about fear—the fear of failure, the fear of criticism, and ultimately, the fear of not being worthy. It pushes us to do more, achieve more, and be more, but it never allows us to rest, to celebrate, or to appreciate our own progress.

The truth is, perfection doesn't exist. It's a mirage that keeps us chasing an ideal we can never reach. Surrendering perfectionism means embracing our humanity, our flaws, and our imperfections. It means showing up as we are, believing that who we are is enough. Today, release one area where you've been holding yourself to an impossible standard. Allow yourself to show up as beautifully imperfect, knowing that in your imperfections, you are perfectly you.

Affirmation
I release my need for perfection and embrace the beauty of my authentic self. I am enough just as I am.

Reflections with Grace

What does perfectionism try to protect you from?
Where in your life could you give yourself
permission to be enough, just as you are?

_____

_____

_____

_____

_____

_____

_____

_____

_____

_____

_____

Day 20 – Embracing Acceptance

Light for Your Path

"Acceptance doesn't mean resignation; it means understanding that something is what it is and that there's got to be a way through it."
— Michael J. Fox

Reflection

Acceptance is often misunderstood as giving up or resigning ourselves to a situation. But true acceptance isn't about surrendering our power; it's about acknowledging reality without resistance. It's the difference between fighting against a closed door and calmly looking for an open window. Acceptance creates space for us to find solutions, learn lessons, and ultimately move forward.

When we resist what is, we create tension, frustration, and suffering. We waste energy wishing things were different, when that energy could be used to respond creatively and constructively. Acceptance doesn't mean you have to like or agree with what's happening. It simply means you stop resisting it. Today, think of one situation you've been resisting. What would it look like to accept it as it is, even if just for today?

Affirmation

I release my resistance and embrace acceptance. I trust that by accepting what is, I open myself to new possibilities.

Reflections with Grace

What have you been resisting that might bring
peace if you accepted it?
How does acceptance create room for healing or
growth in your life?

_____

_____

_____

_____

_____

_____

_____

_____

_____

_____

_____

PART THREE

Releasing Expectations

So much of our pain stems not from what happened, but from what we thought should have happened. In this section, we gently unravel the expectations we've placed on ourselves, others, and life itself. Releasing them isn't defeat—it's freedom. A return to clarity, truth, and spaciousness.

Day 21 – Letting Go of Expectations from Others

Light for Your Path
"Expectations are premeditated resentments."
— Anonymous

Reflection

We all have expectations—of our partners, friends, family, and even strangers. We expect them to understand our needs, act a certain way, or respond in a manner that fits our idea of what's right. But when reality doesn't meet those expectations, resentment and disappointment can set in. We feel let down, not necessarily because of the actions of others, but because of the gap between what we expected and what actually happened.

Letting go of expectations doesn't mean lowering your standards or accepting mistreatment. It means releasing the hold those expectations have over you and giving yourself permission to see people as they are. When you let go of how you think someone should be, you create space for acceptance, for seeing them as they truly are—flaws and all. Today, practice releasing one expectation you have of someone close to you. Allow them to show up as themselves, without judgment or resentment.

Affirmation
I release my expectations of others and choose to see them as they are, with compassion and understanding.

Reflections with Grace

What expectations from others have you carried
that no longer serve you?
How would it feel to define your life on your own
terms instead?

_____

_____

_____

_____

_____

_____

_____

_____

_____

_____

Day 22 – Letting Go of Unrealistic Standards for Yourself

Light for Your Path
"I am not a perfect person. I make a lot of mistakes. But I'm still proud to be me."
— Anonymous

Reflection

We often set the highest, most unrealistic standards for ourselves —standards we wouldn't dream of imposing on anyone else. When we inevitably fall short, we berate ourselves, feeling inadequate and unworthy. We forget that it's okay to make mistakes, to have off days, and to not be the best at everything. Being human means being imperfect, messy, and beautifully flawed.

What would happen if you gave yourself permission to be a beginner, to stumble, to not have it all figured out? Releasing unrealistic standards means acknowledging your humanity and embracing self-compassion. It means celebrating your efforts rather than focusing on where you fell short. Today, think of one standard you've held yourself to that feels unattainable. Let it go, and replace it with the gentle reminder that who you are is enough.

Affirmation
I release the pressure of unrealistic standards and embrace my humanity. I am enough, just as I am.

Reflections with Grace

What self-imposed standards are you ready to release?
How can you offer yourself grace while still growing?

_____

_____

_____

_____

_____

_____

_____

_____

_____

_____

_____

Day 23 – Releasing Expectations Around Timing

Light for Your Path

"Be patient with yourself, nothing in nature blooms all year."
— Anonymous

Reflection

We often have a timeline in our minds for when things should happen—when we should be successful, when we should be married, when we should achieve our goals. When life doesn't follow that timeline, it's easy to feel frustrated and discouraged. But just like nature has its seasons, so do we. Some things need time to grow and develop. Just because it hasn't happened yet, doesn't mean it won't. It just means it's not time.

Letting go of expectations around timing means trusting that everything happens exactly when it's meant to. It's about releasing impatience and surrendering to the flow of life. When we stop pressuring ourselves to hit arbitrary deadlines, we can actually enjoy the journey and appreciate the lessons we're learning along the way. Today, take a deep breath and release your attachment to one specific timeline. Trust that you are exactly where you need to be, and what's meant for you is making its way to you.

Affirmation

I release my expectations around timing and trust that everything is unfolding perfectly. I am exactly where I need to be.

Reflections with Grace

Where in your life are you holding on to a
specific timeline?
What might open up if you trusted divine or natural
timing instead?

Day 24 – Letting Go of Expectations in Relationships

Light for Your Path
"The greatest gift you can give yourself is to free yourself from the expectations of others."
— Anonymous

Reflection
Expectations in relationships can create invisible walls. When we expect our partners, friends, or family to fulfill certain roles or behave in specific ways, we set ourselves up for disappointment and conflict. We may expect our partners to read our minds, our friends to always understand us, or our family to support every decision we make. But these expectations can become chains that restrict both us and them.

Releasing expectations in relationships doesn't mean lowering your boundaries or settling for less. It means allowing others to show up authentically, without projecting your needs onto them. It's recognizing that people can love and support you in their own way, not necessarily the way you envisioned. Today, think about a relationship where you've placed heavy expectations. What would happen if you let go of one of those expectations? How would it feel to allow that person to simply be who they are?

Affirmation
I release my expectations of others in relationships and allow them to show up as their authentic selves. I trust that love grows best in freedom.

Reflections with Grace

What unspoken expectations are you holding in
your relationships?
How might releasing those expectations create
space for more authentic connection?

Day 25 –Letting Go of Expectations of Success

Light for Your Path

"Success is not final, failure is not fatal: It is the courage to continue that counts."
— Winston S. Churchill

Reflection

We all have ideas of what success should look like—career accomplishments, financial stability, recognition. But these external markers of success often come with the pressure to perform, to achieve, and to constantly strive for more. When we don't reach these expectations, we may feel like failures, questioning our worth and abilities. But true success is not about meeting external expectations; it's about growth, learning, and staying true to your values.

What does success mean to you when you strip away society's definitions? Is it peace of mind, fulfilling relationships, a sense of purpose? Today, release one expectation you've placed on yourself around success. Focus on what success feels like rather than what it looks like. Embrace your own definition of success, and let that be your guide.

Affirmation

I release external expectations of success and embrace my own definition of fulfillment. I am successful by being true to myself.

Reflections with Grace

How have you defined success, and who
influenced that definition?
What would it feel like to redefine success in a way that
honors your truth?

_____

_____

_____

_____

_____

_____

_____

_____

_____

_____

Day 26 – Releasing the Need for External Validation

Light for Your Path
"No one can make you feel inferior without your consent."
— Eleanor Roosevelt

Reflection

The need for external validation can be a powerful motivator, but it can also trap us in a cycle of people-pleasing and self-doubt. We seek approval from others—friends, family, colleagues, even strangers—hoping their praise will confirm our worth. But relying on others to validate us gives them power over our self-esteem and happiness. When they approve, we feel good. When they don't, we feel rejected or inadequate.

What if you could validate yourself? What if you knew, deep down, that your worth isn't contingent on someone else's opinion? Releasing the need for external validation means turning inward for approval and trusting your own judgment. Today, think of a recent time when you sought validation from someone else. How would it feel to give yourself that same validation instead?

Affirmation
I release my need for external validation and trust my own worth.
I am enough, just as I am.

Reflections with Grace

In what areas of your life do you still seek
approval from others?
What does it mean to trust your own voice and worth
without outside validation?

Day 27 – Releasing the Expectation to Always Be Happy

Light for Your Path

"Happiness is not a goal...it's a by-product of a life well lived."
— Eleanor Roosevelt

Reflection

The pressure to always be happy can be overwhelming. Social media, self-help books, and even well-meaning friends can give the impression that happiness is the ultimate destination, the end goal of life. But chasing happiness can lead to a never-ending pursuit, leaving us feeling like we're failing when we experience sadness, anger, or grief. Happiness isn't a constant state—it's one of many emotions that ebb and flow.

Letting go of the expectation to always be happy means embracing the full spectrum of human experience. It's about allowing yourself to feel joy and sorrow, excitement and boredom, hope and despair, without labeling any emotion as "wrong." Happiness comes not from avoiding negative emotions but from embracing all of them. Today, release the expectation to feel happy all the time. Allow yourself to experience whatever arises, knowing that all emotions are valid and temporary.

Affirmation

I release the expectation to always be happy. I allow myself to experience the full range of emotions with acceptance and grace.

Reflections with Grace

How have you felt pressured to appear happy, even
when you weren't?
What would it look like to honor your full range of
emotions without judgment?

_____

_____

_____

_____

_____

_____

_____

_____

_____

_____

Day 28 – Releasing the Need for Closure

Light for Your Path

"Sometimes, closure comes not from answers, but from accepting that not all questions need to be answered."
— Unknown

Reflection

The need for closure can keep us stuck, waiting for an explanation, an apology, or some final piece of the puzzle that will make everything make sense. We think that once we have that closure, we'll be able to move on. But closure isn't something that can always be given by someone else—it's a choice we make for ourselves.

Sometimes, the answers we're looking for will never come. The apology will never be spoken. The reason for someone's actions will never be revealed. Holding onto the need for closure only keeps us tethered to the past, reliving pain and waiting for something outside of us to bring peace. Real closure comes from accepting that some things will remain unfinished, and that's okay. Today, choose to release one situation where you've been waiting for closure. Give yourself permission to let go and move forward, trusting that peace comes from within.

Affirmation

I release my need for closure from others and choose to create my own peace. I accept that not everything will be resolved, and I move forward with grace.

Reflections with Grace

Is there a situation in your life where closure may
never come the way you hoped?
What might it feel like to give yourself permission
to move forward anyway?

_____

_____

_____

_____

_____

_____

_____

_____

_____

_____

Day 29 – Letting Go of Judgment

Light for Your Path

"If you judge people, you have no time to love them."
— Mother Teresa

Reflection

Judgment can be a sneaky form of control. We judge others to distance ourselves from their mistakes or shortcomings, hoping to prove that we are different, better, or superior. But judgment is a double-edged sword. The same harshness we direct at others often turns inward, making us our own worst critic. This cycle of judgment prevents us from experiencing true compassion—for ourselves and for others.

What if, instead of judging, we sought to understand? What if we saw mistakes as lessons, not failures? When we let go of judgment, we open our hearts to love and compassion. We see ourselves and others as human, beautifully flawed, and perfectly imperfect. Today, release one judgment you've been holding—whether against yourself or someone else. Replace it with curiosity, kindness, and compassion.

Affirmation

I release judgment and choose compassion. I open my heart to understanding and love.

Reflections with Grace

In what ways do you judge yourself or others that
keep you from feeling free?
How might releasing judgment open you up to
deeper compassion?

Day 30 – Accepting Help Without Guilt

Light for Your Path

"Asking for help isn't weak. It's a strength that shows you understand your own limits."
— Unknown

Reflection

Many of us are taught to be self-reliant, to figure things out on our own and never ask for help. But this belief can create unnecessary struggle and loneliness. Accepting help isn't a sign of weakness or failure—it's a sign of self-awareness and wisdom. It's acknowledging that we all have limits and that there is strength in knowing when to lean on others.

Think of a time when someone reached out to you for help. How did it feel to be trusted and to support someone you care about? Allowing others to help us deepens our relationships and creates a sense of community and connection. Today, release the guilt or shame around asking for help. Allow yourself to be supported, knowing that accepting help is a gift you give to both yourself and others.

Affirmation

I accept help with grace and gratitude, knowing it strengthens both me and my relationships. I am worthy of support.

Reflections with Grace

What beliefs make it difficult for you
to receive support?
How can accepting help be a courageous
act of self-love?

_____

_____

_____

_____

_____

_____

_____

_____

_____

_____

PART FOUR

Finding Strength in Vulnerability

Vulnerability is not a flaw—it's a form of power. Here, you'll lean into the courage it takes to be seen, to need help, and to love yourself as you are. This is the sacred stretch of the journey where softness becomes strength, and truth becomes your guide.

Day 31 – Embracing Vulnerability as Strength

Light for Your Path

"Vulnerability is not winning or losing; it's having the courage to show up and be seen when we have no control over the outcome."
— Brené Brown

Reflection

We're often taught that vulnerability is a weakness, something to be avoided or hidden. But in truth, vulnerability is a sign of immense strength. It takes courage to open ourselves up, to share our fears, dreams, and authentic selves with others, knowing there's a risk we may not be accepted or understood. When we embrace vulnerability, we show up fully, without masks or pretenses.

Vulnerability isn't about oversharing or seeking attention—it's about being honest and real. It's saying, "This is who I am," without fear of judgment. When we allow ourselves to be seen, we build deeper connections with others and create space for real intimacy and growth. Today, think of one area where you've been holding back out of fear of being vulnerable. What would it feel like to let your guard down, even just a little?

Affirmation
I embrace vulnerability as a strength. I choose to show up authentically, knowing that who I am is enough.

Reflections with Grace

When have you allowed yourself to be vulnerable
and felt stronger because of it?
What would it look like to lean into your truth,
even when it feels uncomfortable?

_____

_____

_____

_____

_____

_____

_____

_____

_____

_____

_____

Day 32 – Releasing the Fear of Being Seen

Light for Your Path

"Our deepest fear is not that we are inadequate. Our deepest fear is that we are powerful beyond measure."
— Marianne Williamson

Reflection

There's a paradox to being seen. On one hand, we crave recognition, acknowledgment, and love for who we are. On the other hand, being truly seen can feel terrifying. What if people don't like what they see? What if they reject us, criticize us, or turn away? But hiding yourself away—out of fear of rejection—only diminishes your light and keeps you from shining as brightly as you were meant to.

What if being seen isn't as scary as we imagine? What if it's the key to being accepted, not just by others, but by ourselves? Releasing the fear of being seen means allowing yourself to take up space, to be heard, to be known. It's trusting that your light is worth sharing, even if some people may not understand or appreciate it. Today, choose to let yourself be seen in one small way—whether by sharing your thoughts, your creativity, or simply your presence.

Affirmation
I release my fear of being seen and choose to shine my light brightly.
I am worthy of being known and loved for who I truly am.

Reflections with Grace

What parts of yourself do you still hide from
others, and why?
How might your life shift if you allowed yourself
to be fully seen and accepted?

Day 33 –Letting Go of the Need to Be Strong All the Time

Light for Your Path

"You don't always have to be strong. You don't always have to have it all figured out."

— Anonymous

Reflection

There's a misconception that strength means never breaking, never crying, or never needing help. We think we have to be pillars of resilience, no matter what life throws our way. But this belief only isolates us, keeping us from reaching out when we need support the most. True strength is found in acknowledging our vulnerabilities, in knowing when to rest, and in asking for help without shame.

No one can be strong all the time. It's okay to have moments of weakness, to not have all the answers, or to feel overwhelmed. These moments don't make you any less strong—they make you human. Today, give yourself permission to not be okay. Let go of the expectation that you have to carry everything on your own. Reach out, ask for support, or simply allow yourself to rest.

Affirmation

I release the need to be strong all the time. I embrace my humanity and give myself permission to seek support and rest.

Reflections with Grace

Where in your life do you feel pressured to appear
strong, even when you're not?
What would it feel like to lay that burden down
and ask for support instead?

_____

_____

_____

_____

_____

_____

_____

_____

_____

_____

Day 34 – Allowing Yourself to Receive

Light for Your Path
"We cannot receive what we cannot accept."
— Unknown

Reflection

Being open to receiving—whether it's help, love, or even compliments—requires vulnerability. We may fear being seen as weak or incapable, or we may worry that accepting help will make us indebted to others. But allowing yourself to receive is a gift, both to you and to the giver. It creates a flow of energy, an exchange that deepens connection and trust.

Receiving doesn't diminish your strength; it enhances it. It's an acknowledgment that you don't have to go through life alone. When you allow yourself to receive, you open up to more abundance, love, and joy. Today, when someone offers you help, support, or kindness, practice simply saying "thank you" and receiving it fully, without guilt or reservation.

Affirmation
I am open to receiving love, support, and abundance. I allow myself to be filled with the gifts life offers.

Reflections with Grace

In what ways do you resist receiving—help, love,
compliments, rest?
What would change in your life if you opened
yourself to receive more freely?

_____

_____

_____

_____

_____

_____

_____

_____

_____

_____

Day 35 – Sharing Your True Self

Light for Your Path

"To be yourself in a world that is constantly trying to make you something else is the greatest accomplishment."
— Ralph Waldo Emerson

Reflection

The world often pressures us to fit into certain molds, to be what others expect us to be. We're told to be polite, agreeable, and accommodating, even if it means hiding our true thoughts and feelings. But wearing these masks can leave us feeling unseen, misunderstood, and disconnected from our own identities. Sharing your true self requires vulnerability, but it's also an act of courage and self-love.

Imagine living every day as your authentic self, unafraid of how others may perceive you. You speak your truth, share your ideas, and express your feelings openly. The people who matter will love you for who you are, not for the mask you wear. Today, take one small step toward sharing your true self. Say what's really on your mind, express how you truly feel, or show a side of yourself you've kept hidden.

Affirmation

I share my true self with the world. I am proud of who I am and express my authenticity with confidence and grace.

Reflections with Grace

What parts of yourself do you keep hidden from others?
What would it feel like to show up fully as you are—
without pretense or performance?

_____

_____

_____

_____

_____

_____

_____

_____

_____

_____

Day 36 – Letting Go of Fear of Rejection

Light for Your Path

"Don't be afraid of losing people. Be afraid of losing yourself by trying to please everyone around you."
— Anonymous

Reflection

Fear of rejection can cause us to shrink, to hide our true selves, and to say "yes" when we want to say "no." We want to be accepted, loved, and appreciated, so we bend ourselves to fit others' expectations. But living in fear of rejection means living a life that isn't truly yours. It means sacrificing your authenticity for the approval of others.

Letting go of this fear involves embracing your worth and understanding that rejection is not a reflection of your value. Not everyone will understand or appreciate you, and that's okay. What matters is that you stay true to yourself. Today, take one step toward releasing this fear. Say "no" when you mean no, express your true thoughts, or stand firm in your beliefs, even if it means risking disapproval.

Affirmation

I release my fear of rejection and embrace my authentic self. I am worthy of love and acceptance for who I truly am.

Reflections with Grace

What past experiences have shaped your fear of rejection?
How might your life expand if you no longer let that fear
lead your decisions?

_____

_____

_____

_____

_____

_____

_____

_____

_____

_____

_____

Day 37 – Embracing Your Imperfections

Light for Your Path
"There is a crack in everything, that's how the light gets in."
— Leonard Cohen

Reflection

Perfection is an illusion. It's an unreachable standard that keeps us from fully embracing who we are. Our flaws, our mistakes, our struggles—they are all part of our story, making us unique and beautiful in our own way. When we embrace our imperfections, we allow ourselves to be fully human, to love ourselves not despite our flaws, but because of them.

Imperfections are what make you real and relatable. They're what connect you to others on a deeper level. Today, take a moment to reflect on one of your imperfections that you've been hiding or ashamed of. What if, instead of seeing it as a flaw, you saw it as part of your unique beauty? Release the need to be perfect and celebrate your authentic self.

Affirmation
I embrace my imperfections as part of my unique beauty. I am whole and worthy just as I am.

Reflections with Grace

In what ways have you judged yourself for not
being 'perfect'?
How can you begin to show love and acceptance to
those parts of yourself today?

_____

_____

_____

_____

_____

_____

_____

_____

_____

_____

Day 38 – Releasing the Urge to Compare

Light for Your Path

"Comparison is the thief of joy."
— Theodore Roosevelt

Reflection

It's natural to look at others and see where we measure up. We compare our looks, our careers, our relationships, and even our happiness to the curated images of others. But comparison steals our joy, blinding us to our own blessings and achievements. It creates a sense of lack, making us feel as though we're not enough, no matter how much we have or accomplish.

What would happen if you released the urge to compare? What if you measured yourself only by your own growth, your own progress? Imagine the freedom that would come from embracing your unique path, celebrating your own successes, and appreciating others without judgment or envy. Today, notice when you start to compare yourself to others. Instead, focus on one thing about yourself that you're proud of. Celebrate your own journey.

Affirmation

I release the urge to compare myself to others. I honor my unique path and celebrate my own progress and growth.

Reflections with Grace

Where in your life do you find yourself comparing
your journey to others?
What would it feel like to measure your progress
with compassion instead of comparison?

_____

_____

_____

_____

_____

_____

_____

_____

_____

_____

_____

Day 39 –   Embracing the Power of Silence

Light for Your Path

"Silence is not the absence of sound, but the presence of peace."
— Unknown

Reflection

In a world filled with noise—constant notifications, conversations, and distractions—silence can feel uncomfortable, even intimidating. We rush to fill empty spaces with words, music, or activities. But silence is not something to be feared; it's a powerful tool for finding peace and clarity. In silence, we can hear the whisper of our own thoughts, the rhythm of our breath, and the gentle voice of our inner guidance.

Silence invites us to slow down and connect deeply with ourselves. It's in these quiet moments that we can process our emotions, find solutions, and gain a sense of calm. Today, embrace silence as a practice. Set aside a few minutes to simply sit in silence, without distractions. Notice how it feels to be still, to let the world fade away, and to listen to the quiet within.

Affirmation

I embrace silence as a source of peace and clarity. I allow myself to be still and find calm within the quiet.

Reflections with Grace

When was the last time you allowed yourself
to sit in true silence?
What emotions or insights arise for you in quiet,
unfilled moments?

Day 40 – Honoring Your Emotional Truth

Light for Your Path

"There is no greater agony than bearing an untold story inside you."
— Maya Angelou

Reflection

Honoring your emotional truth means allowing yourself to feel what you feel without apology. It means not minimizing your sorrow or muting your joy to make others comfortable. It means holding space for your experiences, even the ones that don't make sense yet.

In a world that often encourages us to "move on" or "stay strong," honoring your truth is a revolutionary act of care. Whether you're feeling grief, relief, longing, or peace—your emotions are valid.

Today, give yourself permission to sit with what's real for you. You don't have to explain it. You only have to feel it and let it be witnessed—even if only by you.

Affirmation
I honor my emotional truth. I welcome my feelings without judgment and trust the wisdom they carry.

Reflections with Grace

What truth have you been holding back from
yourself or others?
How can you give voice to your real feelings with
compassion and courage?

_____

_____

_____

_____

_____

_____

_____

_____

_____

_____

Beyond the Forty: A Gentle Return to Self

Cultivating Inner Peace and Stillness

These final five reflections are your soft landing. Think of them as an invitation to integrate, settle, and honor how far you've come...

Day 41 – Finding Peace in Solitude

Light for Your Path
"Loneliness expresses the pain of being alone, and solitude expresses the glory of being alone."
— Paul Tillich

Reflection

Being alone often carries a negative connotation. We fear loneliness, associating it with isolation and sadness. But solitude is different—it's a deliberate choice to be with yourself, to hear your own thoughts, and to connect with your inner world. Solitude is an invitation to discover who you are when there's no one else around, to learn to enjoy your own company, and to nurture a deeper relationship with yourself.

In moments of solitude, we find clarity and creativity. It's in these quiet spaces that we can reflect, dream, and reconnect with our true selves. Today, take time to be alone, not out of loneliness, but out of love for your own presence. Allow yourself to just be, without distractions or interruptions. Find the peace that comes from simply sitting with yourself.

Affirmation
I embrace solitude as a time for reflection and self-discovery. I find peace and joy in my own presence.

Reflections with Grace

In what ways does solitude nourish your soul?
How can you create more intentional space for
quiet connection with yourself?

_____

_____

_____

_____

_____

_____

_____

_____

_____

_____

_____

Day 42 – Balancing Effort and Ease

Light for Your Path
"Life is a balance of holding on and letting go."
— Rumi

Reflection

We often operate at two extremes—pushing ourselves too hard or becoming too passive and complacent. We think that success requires constant effort, striving, and doing. But pushing ourselves to the brink only leads to burnout, while doing nothing leaves us unfulfilled. True balance lies in knowing when to push and when to let go, when to put in effort and when to allow ease.

Imagine balancing on a tightrope. Too much force, and you'll tip over. Too little, and you won't move forward. Balancing effort and ease means being in tune with yourself, listening to your body, mind, and spirit. It's about doing what you can and then allowing things to unfold. Today, take note of one area in your life where you're pushing too hard. How can you bring in more ease? How can you find the middle ground between effort and surrender?

Affirmation
I honor the balance between effort and ease. I work with intention and allow space for grace.

Reflections with Grace

Where in your life are you pushing too hard, and
where might you ease up?
How can you invite more grace and flow into your
daily efforts?

_____

_____

_____

_____

_____

_____

_____

_____

_____

_____

Day 43 – Embracing Stillness

Light for Your Path

"Stillness is where creativity and solutions to problems are found."
— Eckhart Tolle

Reflection

In a culture that values constant movement and productivity, stillness can feel unproductive, like wasted time. But stillness is where we find our deepest insights, where creativity blooms, and where solutions arise. It's in stillness that we can hear the whispers of our own intuition and find the answers we've been searching for.

Today, allow yourself a moment of stillness. Whether it's through meditation, a quiet walk, or simply sitting in silence, let go of the need to be doing and simply be. Notice the thoughts, feelings, and inspirations that come when you're not forcing or pushing. Embrace stillness as a source of strength, wisdom, and clarity.

Affirmation

I embrace stillness as a source of clarity and strength. I allow myself to simply be, knowing that in stillness, I find wisdom and peace.

Reflections with Grace

When was the last time you truly sat in stillness
without distraction?
What does stillness reveal to you about your
inner world?

_____

_____

_____

_____

_____

_____

_____

_____

_____

_____

Day 44 – Finding Harmony Within

Light for Your Path

"Peace comes from within. Do not seek it without."
— Buddha

Reflection

We often look outside of ourselves for peace and happiness, believing that once we have the right circumstances, the right job, or the right relationship, we'll finally be at peace. But true peace can't be found in external situations. It comes from within, from cultivating a sense of balance, contentment, and acceptance, no matter what's happening around us.

Finding harmony within means aligning with your own values, staying grounded in your truth, and choosing calm over chaos. It's knowing that you have the power to create peace in any moment by how you respond to life. Today, focus on finding harmony within. When stress or conflict arises, take a deep breath and remind yourself that peace is always available to you.

Affirmation

I find harmony and peace within. I choose calm over chaos and respond to life with grace and balance.

Reflections with Grace

What areas of your life feel out of sync right now?
What small step can you take today to
restore inner balance?

_____

_____

_____

_____

_____

_____

_____

_____

_____

_____

_____

_____

Day 45 – Finding Peace in Letting Go

Light for Your Path

"Some of us think holding on makes us strong; but sometimes it is letting go."
— Hermann Hesse

Reflection

We often think that letting go is a sign of giving up or a lack of strength. But letting go can be one of the most powerful acts of courage and faith. It's choosing to release the grip on what no longer serves us—old beliefs, toxic relationships, unfulfilled dreams—and make space for something new. Letting go doesn't mean erasing the past; it means making peace with it.

Think of one thing in your life that you've been holding onto tightly. Is it serving you, or is it holding you back? What would happen if you released it, trusting that by letting go, you're creating space for growth and new opportunities? Today, practice letting go of one thing, no matter how small. Feel the lightness and freedom that come from releasing what no longer belongs to you.

Affirmation
I am ready to receive love that reflects God's best for me.

Reflections with Grace

What have you been holding onto that
no longer brings peace?
How might releasing it open the door to greater
calm and clarity?

_____

_____

_____

_____

_____

_____

_____

_____

_____

_____

Sacred Rest After Release

For the one who has laid down what once felt too heavy to name...

For the one who finally exhaled...

For the one who dared to loosen their grip — even if only for a moment...

May you rest now in the space you've cleared.

Not in emptiness, but in sacred stillness.

Not in absence, but in quiet return.

May your soul rise, unburdened.

May your breath deepen, steady and free.

May your spirit know it is safe — safe to soften, safe to heal, safe to begin again.

You've done holy work.

You've honored your truth.

You've made space for light.

Let that be enough for now.

You are not behind.

You are not broken.

You are becoming.

So rest, beloved.

Rest in the love that never left you.

Rest in the knowing that release is not the end — it is the gentle threshold of what's next.

The journey continues.

Hope remains.

And so do you.

About the Author

Rita Lynn Berry is a writer, poet, licensed therapist, and spiritual thought leader with over 35 years of experience in counseling and human services. For the past 21 years, she has served as a therapist in private practice, supporting clients through healing, growth, and personal transformation.

Through her signature Journey to Me™ framework, Rita creates devotionals, journals, and reflective tools that invite readers to release what no longer serves, reconnect with their inner wisdom, and return to themselves with love and compassion.

Her work blends emotional insight with soulful reflection—grounded, gentle, and deeply affirming. Letting Go speaks to the practice of release and the quiet power of renewal.

Rita is the founder of Mend n Muse Media and shares daily reflections, affirmations, and creative offerings across social platforms.

Her guiding truth: The journey continues. Hope remains. And so do we.

Connect and explore more:
www.RitaLynnBerry.com
TikTok: @ritalynnberry_1loveword
YouTube: @ritalynnberry
(Search: Journey to Me with Rita Lynn Berry)

www.ingramcontent.com/pod-product-compliance
Lightning Source LLC
Chambersburg PA
CBHW020753130626
46554CB00006B/2167

*9 7 9 8 9 9 9 1 2 2 2 1 5 0 *